THE BIBLE AND SPIRITUAL DISCIPLINES

The Bible and Spiritual Disciplines

inSIGHTS

BIBLE STUDIES FOR GROWING
F A I T H

HOLLY W. WHITCOMB

WIPF & STOCK · Eugene Oregon

Versions of the discussion of the awareness *examen* (39–40) first appeared in *Praying: Spirituality for Everyday Living* 90 (January 15, 1999): 33–34, and in *Ordinary Ministry, Extraordinary Challenge: Women and the Roles of Ministry,* ed. Norma Cook Everist (Nashville: Abingdon, 2000), 38–39. A version of chapter 4, "On Loan to Love," first appeared in *No Other Foundation* (Wisconsin Conference of the United Church of Christ) 15, no. 1 (Summer 1994): 49–52.

Wipf and Stock Publishers
199 W 8th Ave, Suite 3
Eugene, OR 97401

The Bible and Spiritual Disciplines
By Whitcomb, Holly W.
Copyright©2000 Pilgrim Press
ISBN 13: 978-1-60899-218-8
Publication date 1/19/2010
Previously published by Pilgrim Press, 2000

Contents

INTRODUCTION   7

1. FROM HUMAN DOING TO HUMAN BEING: 9
   Sabbath Listening

2. PRACTICING PRAYER'S PERSPECTIVE: 14
   Living a Life of Intercession

3. AN INVITATION TO RELINQUISHMENT AND
   SELF-EMPTYING: 19
   Reclaiming the Fast

4. ON LOAN TO LOVE: 23
   Borrowing and Returning What Is God's

5. DISCOVERING YOUR VOCATION: 29
   Paying Attention to Your God-Given Purpose

6. HOLDING STEADY IN MIDSTREAM: 36
   Nurturing Practices That Keep Us Faithful

NOTES   45

SELECTED BIBLIOGRAPHY   47

Introduction

In my retreat work around the country, I am learning that Christians yearn to talk with one another about living purposefully and faithfully. They ache to travel with companions on their spiritual journeys, to know that they are not alone in their graced moments as well as in their times of trial. In this little book I have focused on six ways of living an intentional and fruitful spiritual life. Each of the six chapters briefly explores a pivotal component of classical Christian spirituality: Sabbath, intercessory prayer, fasting, stewardship, living into one's call, and accountability. The questions at the end of each chapter may be selected and discussed as time permits. May God bless you as you explore your own spiritual disciplines!

HOLLY W. WHITCOMB
Elm Grove, Wisconsin
The Season of Lent

ONE

From Human Doing to Human Being

SABBATH LISTENING

> Stay still for a while.
> Listen.
> Where am I today?
> How is God moving in my life?

If I were asked to name the two most necessary components of my spiritual life, I would instantly reply, "Prayer and Sabbath." I cannot imagine navigating my everyday existence without these two. When I was young, I believed that Sabbath was an unproductive waste of time: good works and hard work seemed to be more effective and more laudable. Now in my middle age, when the quickly evident fruits of non-Sabbath appear in the form of witheredness, weariness, and despair, I am newly in love with the necessity of Sabbath. The motto of Outward Bound reminds me, "If you can't get out of it, get into it!" That's how I feel about Sabbath. For years, to my own detriment, I have tried to get out of Sabbath, so now I'm getting into it and thriving.

Sabbath is a time of deep listening, of rest, of doing nothing — no thing. It is an opportunity to reconnect with ourselves and with our God. There are no shoulds or oughts in Sabbath. It is a time that exists only for itself, a time of being rather than doing.

Tilden Edwards writes:

Not long ago the religion instructor at a Christian high school decided to introduce silent meditation into one of his classes. He gave the students instructions simply to "be" during the silence: to be relaxed and awake, open to life as it is, with nothing to do but appreciate whatever comes. Week by week he slowly increased the amount of time to a maximum of ten minutes.

The student response was very revealing. One boy summarized a general feeling of the class: "It is the only time in my day when I am not expected to achieve something." The response of several irate parents was equally revealing: "It isn't Christian," said one. "I'm not paying all that tuition for my child to sit there and do nothing," proclaimed another.

How is it that ten minutes of silence can be so special and so threatening?[1]

The boy in this story says of the ten minutes of silence, "It is the only time in my day when I am not expected to achieve something." This statement alone is the essence of Sabbath. Sabbath is about practicing stopping in order to live. Sabbath is not about achievement. It is about being.

The commandment to observe Sabbath comes from the Ten Commandments in Exodus. (Yes, it really is in there with the rest of the Ten Commandments. Why do we remember the ones about adultery and covetousness and murder better than this one?) The commandment to observe Sabbath is from Exodus 20:8–11:

Remember the sabbath day, and keep it holy. Six days you shall labor and do all your work. But the seventh day is a sabbath to the LORD your God; you shall not do any work — you, your son or your daughter, your male or female slave, your livestock, or the alien resident in your towns. For in six days the LORD made heaven and earth, the sea, and all that is in them, but rested the seventh day; therefore the LORD blessed the sabbath day and consecrated it.

Orthodox Jews know more about honoring this sense of being rather than doing than we as Christians. To the Jews all the
rest of the week culminates in the richness and renewal of the
Sabbath from sundown on Friday until sundown on Saturday.
Sabbath is not an afterthought, but the crown, the pinnacle
of creation. Sabbath can teach us, as Jews and Christians, a
rhythm between being and doing, grace and drivenness, rest
and work. If we listen, Sabbath can teach us that our identity
does not have to be earned; it is a given from God. It is through
Sabbath that grace and freedom are restored.

We have talked a little about the importance of Sabbath.
Now we ask the question: How do we go about observing Sabbath? Each of you knows in your heart what the best Sabbath
time is for you. You may have practiced a faithful and heartfelt
Sabbath time for years. Traditionally, Sabbath in the Christian
tradition is Sunday. And for some, Sunday worship and Sunday
rest remain gratifying Sabbath experiences. Unfortunately for
many others of us, clergy and lay, Sunday is a day filled with
church business, church responsibilities, or church distrac-
tions. For thousands of people, Sunday is simply another day
to have to show up at work. So it's up to us to live into that
commandment faithfully and to find Sabbath somehow and
somewhere. For one person, the best Sabbath time may be a
long, hot bath each evening. For another person, Sabbath may
mean gathering around the table for a weekly meal with good
friends. For another, Sabbath may be a daily devotional time in
the morning, or perhaps an afternoon time digging in the garden. For others, Sabbath may be a time of walking, reading, or
singing. Whatever Sabbath is, I like to call it *an intentional
time and space for God to enter in.* Donna Schaper calls it
spiritual leisure.[2] Sabbath is a time of re-creation, a time of
remembering who and whose we are.

REFLECTING TOGETHER

- Ask a volunteer to read aloud the Sabbath commandment from Exodus 20:8–11.

- Sing a Song of Sabbath, "Dear God, Embracing Human-kind."[3] The melody is "Rest." How about that? The old hymn name is "Dear Lord and Father of Mankind."

> O sabbath rest by Galilee!
> O calm of hills above!
> There Jesus met you prayerfully;
> the silence of eternity,
> interpreted by love.
>
> Drop your still dews of quietness,
> till all our strivings cease;
> Take from our souls the strain and stress,
> and let our ordered lives confess
> the beauty of your peace.
>
> Breathe through the pulses of desire
> your coolness and your balm;
> Let sense be numb,
> let flesh retire;
> speak through the earthquake, wind, and fire,
> O still, small voice of calm.

- On newsprint, brainstorm everything that comes to mind when you hear the word "Sabbath."

- Read Matthew 11:28–30. What does this mean in the context of Sabbath?

- Put up on newsprint this little list compiled from Donna Schaper's book *Sabbath Sense*:

Sabbath means:

1. humans, being.

2. no shoulds.

3. putting margins on the pages of our days.

4. standing and being still, long enough, that we see into the depth of time.

5. making large out of small, generous out of stingy, simple out of complex.

6. our relief. It is our way out of urgency. It is the turn in the road back to grace.[4]

Which of these statements about Sabbath makes the most sense to you?

- If we define Sabbath as (put on newsprint)

> an intentional time and space
> for God to enter in
> or
> spiritual leisure

where are you finding and observing Sabbath in your life right now? Discuss.

- Sing an old Sabbath song.[5] The words for this Sabbath song were written by John Ellerton, who was born in 1826. Sing it to the tune of "Amazing Grace."

> Behold us, God, a little space
> From daily tasks set free,
> And met within thy holy place
> To rest awhile with thee.
>
> Around us rolls the ceaseless tide
> Of business, toil, and care,
> And scarcely can we turn aside
> For one brief hour of prayer.

TWO

Practicing Prayer's Perspective

LIVING A LIFE OF INTERCESSION

Let us together live a life of intercession.
—letter to Rev. Ed Beers
from Brother Christopher, monk of Taizé

Prayer is more a way of *being*
than an isolated act of doing.
—Tilden Edwards, *Living in the Presence*[6]

On May 7, 1997, I attended a retreat I will never forget. It was called "A Life of Intercession" and was led by my friend and colleague Ed Beers of Madison, Wisconsin. At the end of that rich day, my head and heart were full to bursting. I drove back home pondering that phrase "a life of intercession" over and over again. What would living that kind of life require?

The word "intercessory," as in "intercessory prayer," and the word "intercession" are both based on the Latin verb *intercedere,* which means "to be situated between" or "to be present among." Perhaps we could say then that a life of intercession is a life situated between divinity and humanity, a life made present among the joys and sufferings of others.

I have been pondering the meaning of a life of intercession for some time now. I will be outlining specifically the requirements of a life of intercession as I understand it.

The first requirement of a life of intercession is offering to another the gift of taking time to pray.

Six years ago, long before I attended his retreat, Ed Beers called me from Madison. He said, "Holly, I am making calls about my list of intercessions, and I've been praying for your brother-in-law Bart. How is he doing?" Although Bart had recently died of colon cancer at age forty-two, I realized that Ed Beers had been praying continuously for Bart for a year. Ed inspires me profoundly because he spends at least an hour each day praying on behalf of others. He feels strongly that intercessory prayer is not to be entered into half-heartedly or in a rushed manner, but slowly and fully; he offers this practice of prayer the time it deserves. I never flippantly ask Ed to pray for someone because I know he will devote himself totally to that task.

The second requirement of a life of intercession is trusting in God.

For most of us, this is not an easy step. Do any of us fully comprehend the releasing power of the words "*thy* will be done," which we pray in the Lord's prayer each Sunday? Thy will be done: that means trusting implicitly that God is working alongside us for good, trusting that God's judgment is wiser and deeper than our own. By trusting God, we align our own will with God's will. The beloved scripture from Romans 8 reminds us that "we do not know how to pray as we ought, but ... [the] Spirit intercedes [for us] with sighs too deep for words."

I have learned a great deal about trust in God from my Quaker friends, who when asked to pray, will say simply, "I will hold you in the Light." This prayer of absolute trust, this prayer that delights in God's awesome wisdom, sits in contrast to the highly controlled wish list of desired outcomes that the rest of us frequently present to God. This kind of prayer finds its peace in any outcome that God thinks best. It is a prayer of surrender to the larger picture of God's love.

The third requirement of a life of intercession is living a life of integrity and justice, in other words, walking the talk.

Not long ago, as I was running errands in my neighborhood, I was both amused and perplexed by a huge late model red and gold Cadillac with a vanity license plate that read "Psalm 92."

When I arrived home I decided I needed to brush up on that particular psalm and discovered that it says that the righteous will flourish. The driver of that flashy Cadillac must have felt very righteous indeed. I wonder if the owner of that handsome vehicle was righteous enough to volunteer at a soup kitchen or to help in an inner-city literacy program. A life of intercession means living a life consistent with justice, a life that may entail entering into the sufferings of others. In Isaiah, Yahweh says to the Israelites, "Because there is blood on your hands, I will not listen to your prayer." God does not respect those whose inner life and outer life are not consistent, whose prayer and action remain disconnected. In her book *Dance of the Spirit*, teacher and theologian Maria Harris suggests what she calls "a diet of spiritual nourishment." Included in her diet of spiritual nourishment are weekly participation in a human rights group and one evening a week working for justice.[7] It is through this kind of practice that we come to understand others' needs and gifts as well as our own. When we build a house for Habitat for Humanity, we understand more clearly the needs of the urban poor. When we volunteer for Amnesty International, we begin to grasp what it's like to be a prisoner isolated from the rest of humanity. When we collect pledges and participate in a CROP walk, we know what it feels like to pound the pavement in solidarity with the hungry of the world. During the civil rights movement, activist Daniel Berrigan asked Rabbi Abraham Joshua Heschel, "Why do you march?" Rabbi Heschel responded, "In order to pray."[8]

I have often said that my favorite part of the worship service at my church is what we call "Joys and Concerns." I often weep my way through Joys and Concerns, but it is, nevertheless, the best part. Joys and Concerns is one small way in which I practice living a life of intercession each week. For it is in that time of raising our hands and speaking, and in that time of praying for and with one another, that we learn of our most heartfelt celebrations and fears and struggles. It is in that time of intercession that we commit ourselves to prayer and possibly action as well. Prayer changes the one who prays. If we pray for a person, it is much more likely that we will visit that person in the hospital or take that person a meal. Douglas Steere says, "Whether we intend it or not, to pray for another is to become involved in his or her life. For one who wants to avoid being drawn into costly involvement, intercessory prayer is to be shunned like the plague."[9] Through our intercessions for one another, our horizons are expanded and our worldview changes. It is at that point that our prayer may lead us into action.

To review a bit, we recall that the word "intercession" is based on the Latin verb *intercedere* which means "to be situated between" or "to be present among." The first requirement of a life of intercession is offering to another the gift of taking time to pray. The second requirement of a life of intercession is trusting in God. The third requirement of a life of intercession is living a life of integrity and justice, or walking the talk. To live a life of intercession is to be challenged and is to be blessed.

REFLECTING TOGETHER

- Sing a Song of Intercession, "O Savior, Let Me Walk with You" (formerly "O Master, Let Me Walk with Thee").[10] The melody is "Maryton L.M."

> O Savior, let me walk with you
> in earthly paths of service true;
> Tell me your secret, help me bear
> the strain of toil, the fret of care.
>
> Teach me your patience; let me be
> in closer, dearer company,
> In work that keeps faith sweet and strong,
> in trust that triumphs over wrong.

- Brainstorm on newsprint. What is intercessory prayer?

- The author has called this chapter: "Practicing Prayer's Perspective: Living a Life of Intercession." What does it mean to "practice prayer's perspective"? What perspective does prayer offer?

- The author has written that the first requirement of a life of intercession is offering to another the gift of taking time to pray. How and when do you pray for other people?

- The second requirement of a life of intercession is trusting in God. Whom do you know who demonstrates his or her faith through a profound trust in God? How have you come to know this?

- The third requirement of a life of intercession is walking the talk, living a life of integrity and justice. How are you walking the talk right now? What more would you like to do? Share your ideas.

- The three requirements of a life of intercession as outlined in this chapter are: offering to another the gift of taking time to pray, trusting in God, and finally, walking the talk. What would you add to this list? What other ways might there be to live a life of intercession? Brainstorm on newsprint.

- Sing another verse of "O Savior, Let Me Walk with You":

    In hope that sends a shining ray
    far down the future's broadening way,
    In peace that only you can give,
    with you, O Savior, let me live.

- Read in unison or repeat after the leader line by line this commission by John Wesley:

    Do all the good you can
    By all the means you can
    In all the ways you can
    In all the places you can
    To all the people you can
    As long as ever you can.[11]
    Amen!

THREE

An Invitation to Relinquishment and Self-Emptying

RECLAIMING THE FAST

I humbled my soul with fasting.

—Psalm 69:10

Not long ago I was chatting with a colleague who asked me if I could shed any light on the whole subject of Lent and fasting. First, I called it to his attention that I was much more of a feaster than a faster. Then I shared that fasting, as I understood it, was really a broad summons to abstinence: abstinence from anything to which we are addicted or overly attached. That could be alcohol or sex or food or TV or shopping or busyness, just about anything that we wildly crave and that has some likelihood of preventing us from being whom God created us to be. "Fasting," I said to my friend, "may not imply just giving up food, but anything that makes us crazy and driven and obsessed." In concluding this conversation with my colleague, I asked, "What do you do to excess? What do you think God might be calling you to take a look at?"[12]

Historically, fasting from food (and perhaps water too) has served as an invitation to humility and personal or national repentance. Fasting also has served as an invitation to inner preparedness for a difficult mission, as in the forty-day wilderness fasts of Moses (Deuteronomy 9:9) and Elijah (1 Kings 19:8) and Jesus (Matthew 4:2). Fasting boasts an impressive biblical track record. Some of our favorite characters were faithful fasters: David the king, Esther the queen, Anna the prophetess, Daniel the seer, Paul the apostle.

Today, for many Christians fasting is an invitation to clear-sightedness. When we abstain from something with which we are overly familiar, our vision becomes less cloudy and more penetrating. Once when I was a student in a class for artists, the teacher asked us to refrain from indulging in all forms of media for one week. We were not allowed to read books, magazines, newspapers; we were not permitted to listen to music or radio; we were not allowed to turn on the TV. I did not cope well with this assignment and sheepishly gave up after two days. I was bored to death. It was a sobering spiritual lesson; it had become painfully obvious that I craved constant stimulation.

Through fasting, we identify quickly those things to which we are overly attached, those forces that control us. When we fast we can easily see how addicted we have become to the non-essentials and how that attachment has gotten in the way of a deeper relationship with God. When we fast, we suddenly realize the shallowness of our dependencies and addictions and how far our spiritual selves have migrated from what really counts. When we fast from food, we come to understand how much we rely on certain edible favorites to placate our anger or to soothe our anxiety. When we fast from buying new things, we see how possessing that new item was an attempt to fill another, deeper emptiness. When we abstain from anything, we see clearly all the things we have been substituting for a friendship with God.

Need some clarity? Need to get back in balance? Try fasting.

REFLECTING TOGETHER

- Have you ever fasted from food? If so, for what reason? How did that feel? What did you learn? Discuss.

- Tilden Edwards writes:

    [Fasting] draws us toward simplicity. Further, in my experience the relinquishment of immediate impulses to eat can have a way of reducing the grasping in my mind for all kinds of things. A fallout of this relinquishment...is a less violent mind, one content to just be calmly present without restlessly trying to consume more. A certain sufficiency and ease of the moment emerges. There is room for God to rise lightly in consciousness and for the heaviness of ego to subside.[13]

How does fasting make room for God and push the ego aside? What does Paul mean in Galatians 2:20 when he says, "It is no longer I who live, but it is Christ who lives in me"?

- Marjorie Thompson writes, "The discipline of fasting has to do with the critical dynamic of *accepting those limits which are life-restoring.*"[14] What does Rev. Thompson mean by this? How do you understand limits which are life-restoring?

- (If your group is large, divide into small groups of three or four. Answer these questions, sharing only what is comfortable.) What do you do to excess? To what are you overly attached? How might God help you?

- Come back together in the large group to sing a Song of Perspective, "Jesus Calls Us O'er the Tumult."[15] The melody is "Galilee."

> Jesus calls us, o'er the tumult
> of our life's wild, restless sea;
> Day by day that voice still calls us,
> saying "Christian, follow me."
>
> Jesus calls us from the worship
> of the treasures we adore,
> From each idol that would keep us,
> saying, "Christian, love me more."

- A quotation from Mitch Albom in the bestselling book *Tuesdays with Morrie:*

  > I glanced around Morrie's study. It was the same today as it had been the first day I arrived. The books held their same places on the shelves. The papers cluttered the same old desk. The outside rooms had not been improved or upgraded. In fact, Morrie really hadn't bought anything new — except medical equipment — in a long, long time, maybe years. The day he learned that he was terminally ill was the day he lost interest in his purchasing power.[16]

  How does the clarity induced by illness compare to the clarity induced by a fast? What lessons might be learned from both?

- Ask a volunteer to read aloud the following verse from Deuteronomy 8:3:

  > [God] humbled you by letting you hunger, then by feeding you with manna, with which neither you nor your ancestors were acquainted, in order to make you understand that one does not live by bread alone, but by every word that comes from the mouth of the LORD.

  What does it feel like to receive nourishment from God's word? Discuss.

- Sing two more verses of "Jesus Calls Us, O'er the Tumult":

  > In our joys and in our sorrows,
  > days of toil and hours of ease,
  > Jesus calls, in cares and pleasures,
  > "Christian, love me more than these."
  >
  > Jesus calls us! By your mercies,
  > Savior, may we hear your call,
  > Give our hearts to your obedience,
  > serve and love you best of all.

FOUR

On Loan to Love

BORROWING AND RETURNING
WHAT IS GOD'S

Following on the heels of the chapter about relinquishment, this chapter is also about relinquishment — this time about giving back rather than giving up. This chapter is about the spiritual discipline of stewardship, borrowing and returning what is God's.

This chapter deals with stewardship, but doesn't say much about money. Instead, it focuses on the stewardship of people. Whenever there is a baptism at your local church, you are undoubtedly aware that any new child brought forth is a child of God. Part of each church member's stewardship is taking care of that child for God. As we celebrate the sacrament of baptism, all of us as church members take on the responsibility of being caretakers of that child's life.

For all of us who are parents, it is tempting to believe that it is we who have created our children. When our children look adorable or act precocious or perform clever tricks, we're tempted to murmur proudly, "Just think, I created that child. I must be hot stuff to produce a kid like that." But then we pause and sheepishly remember with awe and wonder the miracle of that child's creation. When we step back and think, we realize that we actually had very little at all to do with that marvelous act. When we're honest, we resonate with the psalmist who writes: "Know ye that the LORD ... is God: it is [God] that hath made us, and not we ourselves ... (KJV). In most stewardship sermons that we hear at church, there is a dominant theme that says: God has given us everything we have and so we are held responsible for taking care of it. Without God we would have nothing. We remember these same words now in this chapter about the stewardship of people. God has given us everything, including all other persons, particularly our children. Just as we do not *own* the land, or the mountains, or the seas, we do not *own* our children. They are ours to borrow for a lifetime, to protect, to educate, to nurture, to care for. They are on loan to love.

In our eagerness, however, to take care of our children, we sometimes forget that we are their caretakers merely until they are old enough to strike out on their own. They belong to God and not to us. We forget that part of the loving is the letting go.

In the last several months, I got a touching calligraphed card from a dear friend who knew I was struggling with letting my children grow up; the card's message read: "There are only two lasting bequests we can hope to give our children. One of these is roots, the other wings." But that gift of wings, that setting free, is never easy, whether it comes as the infant goes off to the babysitter's, as the young child enters kindergarten, as the teenager goes off to college or a job, or as the young adult gets married. It is always tempting to want to possess and hold on. It is never easy to let go.

There is a second kind of stewardship and letting go that we have not yet talked about. That is a letting go to death.

> Sit quietly. Take a moment to remember the last family member's funeral you attended. Recall who that person was who died and what his or her relationship was to you.
>
> At the funeral, what were your feelings inside? How did you feel about that person's dying? How did you feel about God?

Letting go to death is an act of stewardship of the most difficult and radical kind. It is a kind of stewardship that acknowledges that the life of a deceased loved one was never ours to own or to possess in the first place. Letting go to death is a kind of stewardship that remembers that all relationships are a gift from God and that each moment of life spent with the loved one was a bonus and a privilege.

One of the most helpful books I've ever read on letting go to death is a little book called *Tracks of a Fellow Struggler* by John Claypool. John Claypool is an Episcopal priest who shares, through four sermons preached to his congregation, the way he handled, with God's help, the leukemia and death of his ten-year-old daughter, whom he adored. He takes his readers through the personal experience of losing a little girl. He helps us to understand that all of life is a gift. He helps us to grasp what this idea of *on loan to love* is all about. He says:

When World War II started, my family did not have a washing machine. With gas rationed and the laundry several miles away, keeping our clothes clean became an intensely practical problem. One of my father's younger business associates was drafted and his wife prepared to go with him, and we offered to let them store their furniture in our basement. Quite unexpectedly, they suggested that we use their washing machine while they were gone....

Since I used to help with the washing, across the years I developed quite an affectionate relationship for that old green Bendix. But eventually the war ended, and our friends returned, and in the meantime I had forgotten how the machine had come to be in our basement in the first place. When they came and took it, I was terribly upset and I said so quite openly.

But my mother... said, "Wait a minute, son. You must remember, that machine never belonged to us in the first place. That we ever got to use it at all was a gift. So, instead of being mad at its being taken away, let's use this occasion to be grateful that we had it at all."

Here, in a nutshell, is what it means to understand something as a gift and to handle it with gratitude.... I do not mean to say that such a perspective makes things easy, for it does not. But at least it makes things bearable when I remember that [our daughter] was a gift, pure and simple, something I neither earned nor deserved nor had a right to. And when I remember that the appropriate response to a gift, even when it is taken away, is gratitude, then I am better able to try and thank God that I was ever given her in the first place.[17]

In all of our relationships, whether raising a child to adulthood and letting go to life, or in witnessing the death of a husband or wife or child and letting go to death, we thank God for the gift of life. We remember that in all our relationships, whether with our children or with loved ones who have died, we do not own or possess other persons. We merely borrow them and cherish them for the time we are given. From the prologue of the Gospel of John we hear: "All things came into being through [God], and without [God] not one thing came into being." We remind ourselves that we are the stewards not only of the land, the mountains, and the seas, but that we are also stewards of people. It is God that hath made us, and not we ourselves. All persons are gifts to us, temporary gifts, created by God, not for us to own or to possess — but merely on loan to love.

REFLECTING TOGETHER

- Ask a volunteer to read aloud Psalm 8. Ask another volunteer to read aloud Psalm 100. What do these two psalms say about God and creation and stewardship? Discuss.

- Sing a Song of Stewardship, "For the Beauty of the Earth."[18]

> For the beauty of the earth,
> for the splendor of the skies,
> For the love which from our birth
> over and around us lies,

God of all, to you we raise
this our hymn of grateful praise.

For the wonder of each hour
of the day and of the night,
Hill and vale, and tree and flower,
sun and moon, and stars of light,
God of all, to you we raise
this our hymn of grateful praise.

For the joy of human love,
brother, sister, parent, child,
Friends on earth, and friends above,
for all gentle thoughts and mild,
God of all, to you we raise
this our hymn of grateful praise.

- We know as Christians that we do not own the earth, our planet. A popular postcard depicting the earth suspended in space, reminds us: "Good planets are hard to find." How are you being a steward of the earth? How are you protecting God's planet for the generations to come?

- Ask a volunteer to read aloud Numbers 18:25–26, a scriptural admonition to faithful stewardship and tithing. Our Christian tradition has always advocated giving back to God at least one-tenth of what we have been given. What opportunities for spiritual growth does tithing offer us? What opportunities for God's work in the world does tithing provide?

- (If your group is large, divide into small groups of three or four. Answer these questions, sharing only what is comfortable.) What do you think about the stewardship of *people:* not possessing people, but borrowing our loved ones and cherishing them for the time we are given? How are you letting go of loved ones who have grown up? How are you letting go of loved ones who have died?

How does it feel to put relationships in the realm of stewardship?

- Come back together in the large group to sing another Song of Stewardship, "Praise to the Living God."[19] The melody is "Diademata," which you may know as "Crown Him with Many Crowns."

> Praise to the living God,
> the God of love and light,
> Whose word brought forth the myriad suns
> and set the worlds in flight;
> Whose infinite design,
> which we but dimly see,
> Pervades all nature, making all
> a cosmic unity.
>
> Praise to the loving God,
> around, within, above,
> Beyond the grasp of human mind,
> but whom we know as love.
> In these tumultuous days,
> so full of hope and strife,
> May we bear witness to the Way,
> O Source and Goal of life.

FIVE

Discovering Your Vocation

PAYING ATTENTION TO YOUR
GOD-GIVEN PURPOSE

I have called you by name, you are mine.

—Isaiah 43:1b

This chapter is about living into your call, thinking about what your vocation is all about. One popular Bible story about vocation and call is God's call of Samuel taken from 1 Samuel 3:1–10:

Now the boy Samuel was ministering to the LORD under Eli. The word of the LORD was rare in those days; visions were not widespread.

At that time Eli, whose eyesight had begun to grow dim so that that he could not see, was lying down in his room; the lamp of God had not yet gone out, and Samuel was lying down in the temple of the LORD, where the ark of God was. Then the LORD called, "Samuel! Samuel!" and he said, "Here I am!" and ran to Eli, and said, "Here I am, for you called me." But he said, "I did not call; lie down again." So he went and lay down. The LORD called again, "Samuel!" Samuel got up and went to Eli, and said, "Here I am, for you called me." But he said, "I did not call, my son; lie down again." Now Samuel did not yet know the LORD, and the word of the LORD had not yet been revealed to him. The Lord called Samuel again, a third time. And he got up and went to Eli, and said, "Here I am, for you called me." Then Eli perceived that the LORD was calling the boy. Therefore Eli said to Samuel, "Go, lie down; and if he calls you, you shall say, 'Speak, LORD, for your servant is listening.'" So Samuel went and lay down in his place.

Now the Lord came and stood there, calling as before, "Samuel! Samuel!" And Samuel said, "Speak, for your servant is listening."

Most of us who have ever heard this passage about the call of Samuel probably don't remember it very well. When we read the Bible, we tend to recall best those passages that speak to our own lives. At first reading, this story holds little personal appeal. After all, how many of us can truthfully say we have been awakened several times during the night by God's voice? It doesn't happen very often. Samuel's experience may not be our own.

And yet, let us not dismiss this intriguing scripture. We may not have been awakened in the night by the voice of God, but I would guess that most of us have heard God's call somehow and somewhere. Even if we have not received a dramatic summons in the middle of the night, we probably still have some notion of what our call is.

Living into your call: that is what this chapter is all about. Living into your call is one of life's most important spiritual disciplines. Why does it matter? What does it mean?

Perhaps it is easier to think of God's call in terms of vocation. "Vocation" is a word more familiar to us. The word "vocation" comes from the Latin verb *vocare*, which means "to call." Our call, our vocation, is the thread of purposefulness that runs throughout our lives. The theologian Frederick Buechner defines vocation as "the place where your deep gladness and the world's deep hunger meet."[20] Think about that for a moment: *the place where your deep gladness and the world's deep hunger meet.* Our vocation is what we believe God wants us to be doing, our own incomparable contribution as we walk the planet earth.

In living out our vocation, God calls each one of us to be our distinctive and precious self. God does not call us to be someone else. God calls us to be only ourselves, in our rich diversity and uniqueness. Teacher and spiritual writer Parker Palmer says,

> I understand vocation... not as a goal to be achieved but as a gift to be received. Discovering vocation does not mean scrambling toward some prize just beyond my reach but accepting the treasure of the true self I already possess. Vocation does not come from a voice "out there" calling me to become something I am not. It comes from a voice "in here" calling me to be the person I was born to be, to fulfill the original selfhood given me at birth by God.[21]

Years ago when my husband, John, and I used to live in the university community of Iowa City, Iowa, there was a woman known all over town simply as The Elevator Lady. To this day, I have no idea what her real name is. The Elevator Lady was famous, not because she was well educated or held a high-paying job, but simply because she brought joy and cheer into the lives of those around her. The Elevator Lady worked in Mercy Hospital operating the elevator that took the children from the pediatric floor up to surgery. Each day The Elevator Lady would have as her passengers a number of frightened children who were extremely anxious about their upcoming operations. But once on her elevator, the children were talked to, told jokes, giggled with. By the time they got up to surgery, they were smiling and laughing and relaxed.

I share this little story to remind us of the distinction between job and vocation. The Elevator Lady's job was running an elevator at a city hospital. The Elevator Lady's vocation was calming frightened children so they would no longer have to be afraid. A person's job and a person's vocation may be one and the same or they may be different. Knowing what our vocation is helps keep us on track all our lives. If we know what our vocation or call is, and can honor that call, then our lives can continue to be fruitful and joyful and satisfying. The farther we stray from our God-given purpose or vocation, the more distant we become from our true selves. Honoring the true voice of vocation, however, is not always easy.

Here are the stories of two people who have to make decisions regarding their vocations or calls from God. As you hear these stories, ask yourself: How would you respond to the decisions they have to make?

My name is Rob. I've been a family practice physician for fifteen years. I love my job, and I enjoy getting to know my patients and the details of their lives. But my place of work is in a wealthy, upper-middle-class suburb, and I feel God is calling me to spend my time with more needy people. Our family attends a church here on the North Shore, which is a part of a denomination that sends medical missionaries to Africa. The national mission board has asked me if I could sign up for a one-year commitment to help launch a training program. My present place of work will grant me a one-year leave of absence. My wife and my children, five and eleven, will go with me, but they are upset and angry. My wife calls me selfish. Her parents think I've lost my mind and tell me I'm going through a self-absorbed midlife crisis. I would like to go to Africa for just one year. What should I do?

My name is Emily. I have been a lawyer for almost nine years. I became a lawyer because both of my parents were lawyers who worked primarily with rural African-American families in Alabama. As I grew up in the sixties and seventies, I wanted to make a difference in people's lives as I saw my mother and father doing. But now I'm working in an office with ferociously competitive and heartless colleagues with whom I have little in common. I long for a kinder, more gentle environment. The bottom line is that my husband, who is a social worker, left me three years ago. Now I'm a single parent, and I need money to support myself and my three young children. I think I've stayed in this office out of inertia, but now in sixteen months I'll be vested, which means I will get a respectable pension. The day-to-day stress is killing me though, and I'm beginning to become a bitter and cynical person. A friend told me there is an opening for a lawyer to head up a nonprofit organization in our city, but the pay is less than half of that I'm making now. The cost of living here is high and the support of my children is falling mainly on my shoulders. What should I do?

All through our lives each of us has to make our own choices. Those choices are often challenging and demand significant trade-offs. Perhaps right now in your life you may be grappling with personal decisions about vocation. We all have to come up with the answers that are right for us. How are you living into your call right now? What is that thread of purposefulness that runs through your life? What is your vocation?

There is still another facet of the call of Samuel story that we have not yet considered. Samuel does not recognize his call from God when he hears it. Not only does it have to be repeated; it also has to be interpreted for him by another person. It is the old priest Eli who tells Samuel what his call from God is all about. Just as God needed Eli to be Samuel's interpreter, God needs each of us to be ready to interpret. Often in life we can discern another person's call when that person cannot. God calls us to a ministry of encouraging one another. Let me illustrate with a final little story:

There was once a sculptor working hard with his hammer and chisel on a large block of marble. A little boy who was watching him saw nothing more than large and small pieces of stone falling away left and right. He had no idea what was happening. But when the boy returned to the studio a few weeks later, he saw to his great surprise a large, powerful lion sitting in the place where the marble had stood. With great excitement the boy ran to the sculptor and said, "Sir, tell me, how did you know there was a lion in that marble?"[22]

The person who seeks to discern God's call in another is one who knows that there is a lion somewhere in every hunk of marble. Every person has a call and a purpose from God, which often needs to be revealed by patient and loving friends.

Living into your call. That's what this chapter is about. God called Samuel, and God calls each of us. Each of us has been called by God to ministry through the rite and ritual of baptism. A religious call, or vocation, is not just the privilege of priests, nuns, rabbis, and ministers. God calls laymen and laywomen. God calls anyone with ears to hear. We all have a purpose and a vocation. How are you living into God's call?

REFLECTING TOGETHER

- Parker Palmer's book about discovering one's vocation is called *Let Your Life Speak*. How are are you letting your life speak these days? Talk together.

- As we think about our lives, we realize that there is an underlying role that we return to play again and again. My husband knows, for example, that even though he is a physician, he will always be, no matter what, a teacher. I know that I will always be a provider of hospitality. A friend of mine who is a pastor and a preacher names herself first a healer. What is your underlying role? What do you always find yourself returning to do again and again regardless of the particular job you hold? Talk together.

- Writing an epitaph can shed a great deal of light on one's life's purpose. Here is the epitaph of Maggie Kuhn, the founder of the Gray Panthers:

  > Here lies Maggie Kuhn
  > Under the only stone she left unturned.[23]

  How would you write your own epitaph? If you're comfortable doing so, read it aloud.

- (If your group is large, divide into small groups of three or four. Answer these questions, sharing only what is comfortable.) Consider again Frederick Buechner's definition of vocation: "the place where your deep gladness and the world's deep hunger meet." Where does your deep gladness intersect with the world's deep need? What ministry is there for you? What is your call or vocation? How are you living into that call?

- Come back together in the large group to sing a Song of Comfort and Certainty, "O God, Our Help in Ages Past."[24]

> O God, our help in ages past,
> our hope for year to come,
> Our shelter from the stormy blast,
> and our eternal home.
>
> Under the shadow of your throne
> your saints have dwelt secure;
> Sufficient is your arm alone,
> and our defense is sure.
>
> Before the hills in order stood
> or earth received its frame,
> From everlasting you are God,
> to endless years the same.
>
> A thousand ages in your sight
> are like an evening gone,
> Short as the watch that ends the night
> before the rising sun.

- Samuel had Eli to help him to interpret his call from God. Where is your support system? Who helps you to discern your vocation? Share your experiences.

- Stand and gather in a circle, pairing off. (If there is an odd number, one little group of three will stand together.) Bless one another with the words, "God has called you by name. You are God's Beloved."

SIX

Holding Steady in Midstream

NURTURING PRACTICES
THAT KEEP US FAITHFUL

Most of our lives are hectic and demanding. We adhere to tight schedules while being bombarded by the needs of our children, our parents, our co-workers, and our friends. We dwell in a driven "buy, buy, buy" society where we are tempted to believe that who we are is what we own. We cannot remember who we are and whose we are without trying to live with some amount of attentiveness and some amount of accountability. Casinos and bingo halls often post the sign: "You must be present to win." How can we be present to our deeper selves? How can we live as spiritual winners?

Several years ago my husband and I were cleaning out our basement and were ecstatic to discover a seventy-five-year-old Shinto temple bell, which John's missionary grandmother had brought home from Japan. After cleaning it up a bit, we began to play it. This striking temple bell has the same remarkable resonance as the now popular Tibetan singing bowls. Its deep, clear reverberations echo frequently throughout our house. Our spiritual lives reverberate in the same way when we are faithful and when we are accountable.

This chapter sets forth five ways in which we can continue to be accountable:

1. We can worship in a faith community.

2. We can go on retreat.

3. We can keep ourselves steady each day through the use of a daily inventory or examination of conscience.

4. We can live by a personal rule.

5. We can meet regularly with a spiritual director.

We can worship in a faith community.

I'm not one that buys that line, "I can just as easily worship God out on the golf course." I like to play golf too, but I sure can tell the difference between a game of golf and going to church. Communal worship stretches us, challenges us, comforts us, and connects us. We read in the Gospel of Matthew: "For where two or three are gathered in my name, I am there among them." When we go to church, we know that we are part of a community. When we sing hymns together, when we participate in intercessory prayer, when we share our faith stories in Sunday School or Bible Study, we know that we are not alone. We experience the undergirding of mutual support and the kinship of those who depend on God's grace. The hilarious and often poignant author Anne Lamott has a chapter in her spiritual autobiography, *Traveling Mercies*, called "Why I Make Sam Go to Church." When she writes about why she wants her young son to be a part of a faith community she says:

> The main reason is that I want to give him what I found in the world, which is to say a path and a little light to see by. Most of the people I know who have what I want — which is to say, purpose, heart, balance, gratitude, joy — are people with a deep sense of spirituality. They are people in community, who pray, or practice their faith.... They follow a brighter light than the glimmer of their own candle; they are part of something beautiful. I saw something once from the Jewish Theological Seminary that said, "A human life is like a single letter of the alphabet. It can be meaningless. Or it can be a part of a great meaning." Our funky little church is filled with people who are working for peace and freedom, who are out there on the streets

and inside praying, and they are home writing letters, and they are at the shelters with giant platters of food.[25]

Church helps us to be a part of something larger than ourselves.

We can go on retreat.

Retreats offer us an opportunity to ponder our relationship with ourselves, our loved ones, and with God in a place away. Mark 6 tell us:

> The apostles gathered around Jesus, and told him all that they had done and taught. He said to them, "Come away to a deserted place all by yourselves and rest a while." For many were coming and going, and they had no leisure even to eat. And they went away in the boat to a deserted place by themselves.

Retreats offer us a respite from that which is overly familiar and routine. The dictionary defines "retreat" as "the act of withdrawing," or "a place of refuge." On retreat, we have a chance to stand back and to regard our lives from a fresh perspective. Along with that fresh perspective come new inspirations and new resolves.

Retreats abound. There are silent retreats, preached retreats, experiential retreats. They can be a day long or a month long or anything in between. Getting away overnight for at least a day or two can be particularly helpful.

Retreats are marvelously and unpredictably renewing. The Holy Spirit often speaks to us on retreat, because it is there particularly that we are vulnerable and available and open. Consider becoming familiar with the retreats being offered by your own church or denomination or at the conference centers, colleges, convents, or monasteries near your home. Make some calls. Get on some mailing lists. Try committing yourself to a retreat day each month or several overnight retreats each year.

We can keep ourselves steady each day through the use of a daily inventory or examination of conscience.

> Search me, O God, and know my heart;
> test me and know my thoughts.
> —Psalm 139:23

I am a parent of teenage children, a clergywoman, a wife, a spiritual director, a retreat leader, a cook, a soccer mom, and a school volunteer. And sometimes I don't cope very well with the stress of it all. I rely on my daily inventory to add sanity, stability, and a sense of reconnection with God's grace.

The awareness *examen,* or inventory, known by various names in the Christian tradition (daily *examen,* examination of conscience, examination of consciousness) is an ancient and reputable spiritual tool that serves to keep us accountable to ourselves and to God. Such historical figures as Seneca, Pythagoras, Antony of the Desert, Chrysostom, and Basil all advocated use of the *examen.* The practice experienced a resurgence of popularity through St. Ignatius of Loyola (1491–1556) in his *Spiritual Exercises.*

This daily inventory that I created for myself offers me a framework for reflection and prayer twice a day, once in the morning and once at night. It goes like this:

Morning Questions to Start the Day

1. What is my intention for this day? How do I wish to conduct myself?

2. How might God be asking me to let go?

3. Where do I seek God's wisdom and guidance?

Evening Questions to End the Day

1. What have been my sources of grace for this day? For what do I give thanks?

2. For what do I repent?

This is the awareness *examen,* the daily inventory I created for myself. I rely on the fact that it is flexible and that I can omit certain questions or add pertinent new ones at any time. Last week I added a fourth question to my morning inventory: "What is God inviting me into?"

Perhaps you may want to reflect on your own spiritual challenges and create your own daily inventory. It is an insightful tool that has worked well for me.

We can live by a personal rule.

A personal rule is a set of ethical guidelines, a list of spiritual disciplines by which we seek to live. If we abide faithfully by a personal rule, we may be, as Psalm 1 promises, "like trees planted by streams of water." The ultimate example of a personal rule is the Rule of St. Benedict, written in sixth-century Italy, which continues to be the code of spiritual conduct for Benedictine communities around the world today. Personal rules, however, are as uniquely varied as the individuals who create them.

Here are two examples of personal rules. The first is that of Donna Schaper, United Church of Christ minister and prolific author:

1. To meditate on the word "enough."

2. To make a Sabbath effort to play at my work and to work at my play.

3. To connect my inner life to my outer life.

4. To meditate on the meaning of the Christian creed that promises the resurrection of the body and life everlasting. To consider the paradox of becoming more youthful over time.

5. To try to understand the sacrament of marriage as deeply as I can: as a nest and hope for my family and my deepest personal connection to others.[26]

The second example of a personal rule is that required for membership in the Church of the Savior in Washington, D.C.:

1. To spend one hour a day in prayer, meditation, and devotional reading.

2. To worship with the gathered community once a week.

3. To participate in a mission group that is responsive to the claims of the poor.

4. To tithe one's gross income as a basis for "proportional" sharing of one's livelihood.[27]

As you can tell by just these two examples, personal rules vary a great deal. Think about what kinds of values and ideals you've been embracing these last few years. Are you comfortable with those? Would you like to lay out a few new intentions for yourself?

We can meet regularly with a spiritual director.

What is a spiritual director? A spiritual director or spiritual friend is a companion with whom we meet regularly to talk about the perceived presence or absence of God in our lives. The ancient practice of spiritual direction is an ongoing relationship in which a person who wishes to be attentive to his or her spiritual life meets with another person, usually once a month for an hour. Rose Mary Dougherty, faculty member at the Shalem Institute for Spiritual Formation, likes to quote an African proverb when defining this relationship: "It is because one antelope will blow the dust from the other's eyes that two antelopes walk together." A spiritual director listens to us with empathy, cares for us, prays for us, and helps us to sort out divine stirrings amid the substance of our lives, always posing the question: Where is God in all this?

All spiritual directors in the Christian tradition acknowledge that God or Jesus or the Holy Spirit is the true source or guide in all spiritual direction meetings. The spiritual director is merely a midwife or stagehand ushering in an awareness of God's activity and guidance.

What should you look for in a spiritual director?

1. A person who is spiritually mature yet does not pretend to have all the answers.

2. A person who relies on the grace of God.

3. A person who is a perceptive and attentive listener who holds in confidence your sacred story.

4. A person who nurtures his or her own spiritual life.

5. A person who will hold you in prayer.

   If you are thinking you would like some consistent companionship on your spiritual journey, consider meeting regularly with a spiritual friend.

Reflecting Together

- In this chapter, the author describes five ways in which we might be accountable:

  1. We can worship in a faith community.

  2. We can go on retreat.

  3. We can keep ourselves steady each day through the use of a daily inventory or examination of conscience.

  4. We can live by a personal rule.

  5. We can meet regularly with a spiritual director.

  Which of these ways of being accountable have you already experienced? Which ones might you like to explore? Discuss.

- Sing a song of God's Companionship, two verses of "Be Now My Vision" (formerly "Be Thou My Vision").[28] The melody is "Slane."

  > Be now my vision, O God of my heart;
  > nothing surpasses the love you impart —
  > You my best thought, by day or by night,
  > waking or sleeping, your presence my light.

> Be now my wisdom, and be my true word;
> ever within me, my soul is assured;
> Mother and Father, you are both to me,
> now and forever your child I will be.

- Talk about retreat experiences. Who in the room has gone on retreat? What kind of retreat? How did it feel to have that kind of time and space apart? Discuss.

- Ask a volunteer to read aloud the excerpt from Anne Lamott about why she makes her young son, Sam, go to church. What is church to you? What does it mean to you to worship in a faith community?

- Ask a volunteer to read what might be considered Jesus Christ's own personal rule, Mark 12:28–31. Next ask a volunteer to read aloud author Donna Schaper's personal rule. Finally, ask a third person to read aloud the personal rule from the Church of the Savior. Hand out pencils and paper. Invite each person to sit quietly for fifteen minutes and to reflect on what his or her own personal rule might be. Invite any willing persons to read their personal rules aloud.

- (If your group is large, divide into small groups of three or four. Answer these questions, sharing only what is comfortable.) When you think of the word "accountability" in connection with your spiritual life, what does that mean to you? To what or to whom are you accountable on a regular basis? Is there anything in your accountability with regard to your spiritual life that you would like to change?

- Come back together in the large group to sing two more verses of "Be Now My Vision."

> Riches I need not, nor life's empty praise,
> you, my inheritance, now and always;
> You and you only are first in my heart,
> great God, my treasure, may we never part.

Sovereign of heaven, my victory won,
may I reach heaven's joys, O bright heaven's Sun!
Heart of my own heart, whatever befall,
still be my vision, O Ruler of all.

Notes

One: From Human Doing to Human Being

1. Tilden Edwards, *Spiritual Friend: Reclaiming the Gift of Spiritual Direction* (New York: Paulist Press, 1980), 69.

2. Donna Schaper, *Sabbath Sense: A Spiritual Antidote for the Overworked* (Philadelphia: Innisfree Press, 1997), 14.

3. From *The New Century Hymnal* (Cleveland: The Pilgrim Press, 1995), 502. Copyright © 1995 The Pilgrim Press. Used by permission.

4. Schaper, *Sabbath Sense*, 52, 14, 63, 119, 16, 79.

5. Adapted from *The Pilgrim Hymnal* (Boston: The Pilgrim Press, 1931), 395. Copyright © 1931, 1935, 1958; renewed 1986 by The Pilgrim Press. Used by permission.

Two: Practicing Prayer's Perspective

6. Tilden Edwards, *Living in the Presence: Disciplines for the Spiritual Heart* (San Francisco: Harper & Row, 1987), 11.

7. Maria Harris, *Dance of the Spirit: The Seven Steps of Women's Spirituality* (New York: Bantam, 1989), 137.

8. Edwin Beers, "A Seamless Garment," *Spirit Unfolding* (Winter 1997): 2.

9. Douglas V. Steere, "Intercession: Caring for Souls," *Weavings* 4, no. 2 (March/April 1989): 22.

10. From *The New Century Hymnal*, 503. Used by permission.

11. M. J. Ryan, ed., *A Grateful Heart* (Berkeley, Calif.: Conari Press, 1994), 29.

Three: An Invitation to Relinquishment and Self-Emptying

12. See Marjorie J. Thompson, *Soul Feast: A Invitation to the Christian Spiritual Life* (Louisville: Westminster John Knox, 1995).

13. Edwards, *Living in the Presence*, 31.

14. Thompson, *Soul Feast*, 74.

15. From *The New Century Hymnal*, 172. Copyright © 1995 The Pilgrim Press. Used by permission.

16. Mitch Albom, *Tuesdays with Morrie: An Old Man, a Young Man, and Life's Greatest Lesson* (New York: Doubleday, 1997), 125.

Four: On Loan to Love

17. John Claypool, *Tracks of a Fellow Struggler: How to Handle Grief* (Waco, Tex.: Word Books, 1974), 75–76.

18. From *The New Century Hymnal*, 28. Copyright © 1995 The Pilgrim Press. Used by permission.

19. From *The New Century Hymnal*, 8. Words copyright © 1966 by the Estate of Curtis Beach. Used by permission.

Five: Discovering Your Vocation

20. Frederick Buechner, *Wishful Thinking: A Seeker's ABC* (San Francisco: HarperSanFrancisco, 1993), 119.

21. Parker J. Palmer, *Let Your Life Speak: Listening for the Voice of Vocation* (San Francisco: Jossey-Bass Publishers, 2000), 10.

22. Henri J. M. Nouwen, *Clowning in Rome* (Garden City, N.Y.: Doubleday, 1979), 87.

23. Richard L. Morgan, *Remembering Your Story: A Guide to Spiritual Autobiography* (Nashville: Upper Room Books, 1996), 136.

24. From *The New Century Hymnal*, 25. Copyright © 1995 The Pilgrim Press. Used by permission.

Six: Holding Steady in Midstream

25. Anne Lamott, *Traveling Mercies: Some Thoughts on Faith* (New York: Pantheon, 1999), 100.

26. Schaper, *Sabbath Sense*, 36.

27. Dorothy C. Bass, ed., *Practicing Our Faith: A Way of Life for a Searching People* (San Francisco: Jossey-Bass, 1997), 57–58.

28. From *The New Century Hymnal*, 451. Word alterations copyright © 1992 The Pilgrim Press. Used by permission.

Selected Bibliography

Albom, Mitch. *Tuesdays with Morrie: An Old Man, a Young Man, and Life's Greatest Lesson.* New York: Doubleday, 1997.

Bass, Dorothy C., ed. *Practicing Our Faith: A Way of Life for a Searching People.* San Francisco: Jossey-Bass, 1997.

Beers, Edwin. "A Life of Intercession." *Spirit Unfolding* (Winter 1999): 1–3.

Bohler, Carolyn Stahl. *Prayer on Wings: A Search for Authentic Prayer.* San Diego: LuraMedia, 1990.

Claypool, John. *Tracks of a Fellow Struggler: How to Handle Grief.* Waco, Tex.: Word Books, 1974.

Edwards, Tilden. *Spiritual Friend: Reclaiming the Gift of Spiritual Direction.* New York: Paulist Press, 1980.

———. *Living in the Presence: Disciplines for the Spiritual Heart.* San Francisco: Harper & Row, 1987.

———. *Sabbath Time.* Nashville: Upper Room Books, 1992.

Foster, Richard J. *Celebration of Discipline: The Path to Spiritual Growth,* revised edition. San Francisco: Harper & Row, 1988.

Harris, Maria. *Dance of the Spirit: The Seven Steps of Women's Spirituality.* New York: Bantam, 1989.

Heschel, Abraham Joshua. *The Sabbath: Its Meaning for Modern Man.* New York: Noonday Press, 1951.

Kornfield, Jack. *A Path with Heart: A Guide through the Perils and Promises of Spiritual Life.* New York: Bantam, 1993.

Lamott, Anne. *Traveling Mercies: Some Thoughts on Faith.* New York: Pantheon, 1999.

Morgan, Richard L. *Remembering Your Story: A Guide to Spiritual Autobiography.* Nashville: Upper Room Books, 1996.

The New Century Hymnal. Cleveland: The Pilgrim Press, 1995.

Palmer, Parker J. *Let Your Life Speak: Listening for the Voice of Vocation.* San Francisco: Jossey-Bass, 2000.

Remen, Naomi Rachel. *Kitchen Table Wisdom: Stories That Heal.* New York: Riverhead Books, 1996.

Schaper, Donna. *Sabbath Sense: A Spiritual Antidote for the Overworked.* Philadelphia: Innisfree Press, 1997.

Steere, Douglas V. "Intercession: Caring for Souls." *Weavings* 4, no. 2 (March/April 1989): 16–25.

Thompson, Marjorie J. *Soul Feast: An Invitation to the Christian Spiritual Life.* Louisville: Westminster John Knox, 1995.

Warford, Malcolm. *Our Several Callings: A Foundation Paper on Vocation as a Lifelong Issue for Education.* Cleveland: Division of Education and Publication, United Church Board for Homeland Ministries, 1990.

Whitcomb, Holly W. *Feasting with God: Adventures in Table Spirituality.* Cleveland: United Church Press, 1996.

About the Author

HOLLY WILSON WHITCOMB has been a pastor and clergywoman in the United Church of Christ since her graduation from Yale Divinity School in 1978 and has served churches in Connecticut, Iowa, and Wisconsin. She is also a graduate of the two-year training program for spiritual directors at the Shalem Institute for Spiritual Formation in Bethesda, Maryland. As the director of Kettlewood Retreats, Holly is a retreat leader and spiritual director who travels to churches, retreat houses, and conference centers all over the country. She is the author of numerous articles on spirituality as well as the book *Feasting with God*. She lives in a suburb of Milwaukee, Wisconsin, with her husband, John, and their two children, David and Kate.

Holly Whitcomb can be reached at the Kettlewood Retreats Office (262-784-5593) or by e-mail at chota@execpc.com.